Get Your Loans Approved!

Unbelievably Easy and Legal Ways to Improve Your Credit Score

By: Kimberly Green

9781635012781

PUBLISHERS NOTES

Disclaimer – Speedy Publishing LLC

This publication is intended to provide helpful and informative material. It is not intended to diagnose, treat, cure, or prevent any health problem or condition, nor is intended to replace the advice of a physician. No action should be taken solely on the contents of this book. Always consult your physician or qualified health-care professional on any matters regarding your health and before adopting any suggestions in this book or drawing inferences from it.

The author and publisher specifically disclaim all responsibility for any liability, loss or risk, personal or otherwise, which is incurred as a consequence, directly or indirectly, from the use or application of any contents of this book.

Any and all product names referenced within this book are the trademarks of their respective owners. None of these owners have sponsored, authorized, endorsed, or approved this book.

Always read all information provided by the manufacturers' product labels before using their products. The author and publisher are not responsible for claims made by manufacturers.

This book was originally printed before 2014. This is an adapted reprint by Speedy Publishing LLC with newly updated content designed to help readers with much more accurate and timely information and data.

Speedy Publishing LLC

40 E Main Street, Newark, Delaware, 19711

Contact Us: 1-888-248-4521

Website: http://www.speedypublishing.co

REPRINTED Paperback Edition: 9781635012781:

Manufactured in the United States of America

DEDICATION

I dedicate this book to the greatest financial adviser ever - my husband, Scott.

TABLE OF CONTENTS

CHAPTER 1 - WHAT IS CREDIT REPAIR?

Credit Repair is defined as a method of disputing or rectifying discrepancies presented on credit bureau reports in order to obtain the highest and most exact ratings for consumers.

Among the most crucial matters to think back is regarding credit problems and this also means you're not the only one who is suffering from bad credit. On the other side, there are millions of honorable, hard-working people from all around the country who are presently experiencing or have suffered troubles with their credit too. However, your awareness of the importance of having good credit has put you one step closer to actually achieving a good credit rating and improving your quality of living.

Even though your credit rating may seem like an intangible asset, it is one of the most valuable and important assets that you have. Without a good credit rating your financial, occupational, and personal goals are at risk of being severely limited. In order to obtain the privilege of using a credit card, your credit rating is checked.

Get Your Loans Approved!

If a company determines your credit to be unsatisfactory, you will be denied. From the moment you are denied, your quality of living is impeded. If you can't get a credit card, you can't rent a car, order tickets, or even rent a video. Because your credit rating was determined to be unsatisfactory, most companies will not let you use their money.

Today more than ever, many businesses perform routine background checks during the hiring process. Once again, if your credit rating reveals something of concern to them, you can be turned away for employment.

Since maintaining a good credit rating is important in today's society, a poor credit rating can have a negative snowball effect toward your personal goals. Good, string credit allows you to live with financial security and enables you to purchase items without depleting your life savings.

Repairing your credit can seem like a monumental task; however, it can also be as easy as wiring a letter or making a phone call. Your decision to repair your credit rating will benefit you for the rest of your life.

The more time you invest now toward strengthening your credit rating, the better your quality of life will be.

The Origin and Importance of Your Credit Score

Before you start boosting your credit score, you need to know the basics. You need to know what a credit score is, how it is developed, and why it is important to you in your everyday life.

Lenders certainly know what sort of information they can get from a credit score, but knowing this information yourself can help you better see how your everyday financial decisions impact the financial picture lenders get of you through your credit score. A few simple tips are all you need to know to understand the basic principles:

Understand where credit scores come from

If you are going to improve your credit score, then logic has it that you must understand what your credit score is and how it works. Without this information, you won't be able to very effectively improve your score because you won't understand how the things you do in daily life affect your score. If you don't understand how your credit score works, you will also be at the mercy of any company that tries to tell you how you can improve your score - on their terms and at their price.

In general, your credit score is a number that lets lenders know how much of a credit risk you are. The credit score is a number, usually between 300 and 850, that lets lenders know how well you are paying off your debts and how much of a credit risk you are. The higher your credit score, the better credit risk you make and the more likely you are to be given credit at great rates. Scores in the low 600s and below will often give you trouble in finding credit, while scores of 720 and above will generally give you the best interest rates out there. However, credit scores are a lot like GPAs or SAT scores from college days - while they give others a quick snapshot of how you are doing, they are interpreted by people in different ways. Some lenders put more emphasis on credit scores than others.

Some lenders will work with you if you have credit scores in the 600s, while others offer their best rates only to those creditors with very high scores indeed. Some lenders will look at your entire credit report while others will accept or reject your loan application based solely on your credit score.

The credit score is based on your credit report, which contains a history of your past debts and repayments. Credit bureaus use computers and mathematical calculations to arrive at a credit score from the information contained in your credit report. Each credit bureau uses different methods to do this (which is why you will have different scores with different companies) but most credit bureaus use the FICO system. FICO is an acronym for the credit score calculating software offered by Fair Isaac Corporation. This is by far the most used software since the Fair Isaac Corporation developed the credit score model used by many in the financial industry and is still considered one of the leaders in the field.

In fact, credit scores are sometimes called FICO scores or FICO ratings, although it is important to understand that your score may be tabulated using different software. One other thing you may want to understand about the software and mathematics that goes into your credit score is the fact that the math used by the software is based on research and comparative mathematics. This is an important and simple concept that can help you understand how to boost your credit score. In simple terms, what this means is that your credit score is in a way calculated on the same principles as your insurance premiums.

Your insurance company likely asks you questions about your health, your lifestyle choices (such as whether you are a smoker) because these bits of information can tell the insurance company how much of a risk you are and how likely you are to make large claims later on. This is based on research. Studies have shown, for example, that smokers tend to be more prone to serious illnesses and so require more medical attention. If you are a smoker, you may face higher insurance premiums because of this.

Kimberly Green

Similarly, credit bureaus and lenders often look at general patterns. Since people with too many debts tend not to have great rates of repayment, your credit score may suffer if you have too many debts, for example. Understanding this can help you in two ways:

1) It will let you see that your credit score is not a personal reflection of how "good" or "bad" you are with money. Rather, it is a reflection of how well lenders and companies think you will repay your bills - based on information gathered from studying other people.

2) It will let you see that if you want to improve your credit score, you need to work on becoming the sort of debtor that studies have shown tends to repay their bills. You do not have to work hard to reinvent yourself financially and you do not have to start making much more money. You just need to be a reliable lender. This realization alone should help make credit repair far less stressful!

Credit reports are put together by credit bureaus, which use information from client companies. It works like this: credit bureaus have clients - such as credit card companies and utility companies, to name just two - who provide them with information. Once a file is begun on you (i.e. once you open a bank account or have bills to pay) then information about you is stored on the record. If you are late paying a bill, the clients call the credit bureaus and note this. Any unpaid bills, overdue bills or other problems with credit count as "dings" on your credit report and affect your score. Information such as what type of debt you have, how much debt you have, how regularly you pay your bills on time, and your credit accounts are all information that is used to calculate your credit score.

Your age, sex, and income do not count towards your credit score. The actual formula used by credit bureaus to calculate credit scores

Get Your Loans Approved!

is a well-kept secret, but it is known that recent account activity, debts, length of credit, unpaid accounts, and types of credit are among the things that count the most in tabulating credit scores from a credit report.

Keep the contact information for credit bureaus handy

The three major credit bureaus are important to contact if you are going to repair your credit score. The major three credit agencies can help you by sending you your credit report. If you find an error on your credit report, these are also the companies you must contact in order to correct the problem. You can easily contact these organizations by mail, telephone, or through the Internet: Equifax Credit Information Services, Inc., TransUnion LLC Consumer Disclosure Center and Experian National Consumer Assistance Center.

You may want to note this information wherever most of your financial information is kept so that you can easily contact the bureaus whenever you need to. Your local yellow pages should also have the contact information of these credit agencies as well.

Develop an action plan for dealing with your credit score

Once you have your credit report and your credit score, you will be able to tell where you stand and where many of your problems lie. If you have a poor score, try to see in your credit report what could be causing the problem:

- -Do you have too much debt?
- -Too many unpaid bills?
- -Have you recently faced a major financial upset such as a bankruptcy?

- -Have you simply not had credit long enough to establish good credit?
- -Have you defaulted on a loan, failed to pay taxes, or recently been reported to a collection agency?

The problems that contribute to your credit problems should dictate how you decide to boost your credit score. As you read through this eBook, highlight or jot down those tips that apply to you and from them develop a checklist of things you can do that would help your credit situation improve. When you seek professional credit counseling or credit help, counselors will generally work with you to help you develop a personalized strategy that expressly addresses your credit problems and financial history. Now, with this eBook, you can develop a similar strategy on your own - in your own time and at your own cost.

When developing your action plan, know where most of your credit score is coming from:

1) Your credit history (accounts for more than a third of your credit score in some cases). Serves as an indicator of how you will react to debt in the future. For this reason, late payment, loan defaults, unpaid taxes, bankruptcies, and other unmet debt responsibilities will count against you the most. You can't do much about your financial past now, but starting to pay your bills on time - starting today - can help boost your credit score in the future.

2) Your current debts (accounts for approximately a third of your credit score in some cases). If you have lots of current debt, it may indicate that you are stretching yourself financially thin and so will have trouble paying back debts in the future. If you have a lot of money owing right now - and especially if you have borrowed a great deal recently - this fact will bring down your credit score. You

can boost your credit score by paying down your debts as far as you can.

3) How long you have had credit (accounts for up to 15% of your credit score in some cases). If you have not had credit accounts for very long, you may not have enough of a history to let lenders know whether you make a good credit risk. Not having had credit for a long time can affect your credit score. You can counter this by keeping your accounts open rather than closing them off as you pay them off.

4) The types of credit you have (accounts for about one tenth of your credit score, in most cases). Lenders like to see a mix of financial responsibilities that you handle well. Having bills that you pay as well as one or two types of loans can actually improve your credit score. Having at least one credit card that you manage well can also help your credit score.

As you can see, it is possible to only estimate how much a specific area of your credit report affects your credit score. Nevertheless, keeping these five areas in mind and making sure that each is addressed in your personalized plan will go a long way in making sure that your personalized credit repair plan is comprehensive enough to boost your credit effectively.

Why Did You Get a Bad Credit Rating?

The bad credit situation is the worst situation in the life of a credit card holder. This not only hampers your present life, but also affects your future prospective of securing a loan. The discussion below will inform you about the factors leading to this situation and the strategies to come out of it or never get into it. Factors Leading to Bad Credit Situation

There is no one reason for getting into a bad credit rating. Following are the root causes of this: • Overspending is the most crucial factor that leads to the situation of bad credit. • The inevitable conditions like health problems, unemployment and other financial setbacks also add to the bad credit score. In these circumstances you have to spend without taking care of your credit score. • Non-payment on time for various purchases also affects the credit history.

Why Do You Need Good Credit?

With today's society becoming more and more business oriented, establishing and maintaining good credit is vital if you plan to do any of the following:

- Apply for employment
- Rent an apartment
- Open a bank account
- Setup an account with public service or the telephone company

It used to be that establishing good credit was important only if you planned to buy a home or car, but not anymore. The simplest task, such as applying for employment could very much mean that you need a good credit.

Having bad credit could impede your ability to survive. This is sad to say, but it is a proven fact that people have been turned down top quality job positions just because of their credit rating despite the fact that that particular job could be exactly what a person needs to fix their credit. That's a scary catch twenty-two don't you think?

Ok, I'm caught in that scary catch twenty-two, what should I do?

Get Your Loans Approved!

Start by requesting a copy of your credit report in writing. You are entitled by Federal Law to receive a free annual credit report. There are three major credit-reporting agencies that you need to contact, you can run a search on the internet or find their information in a phone book. If you have already received a credit report for that year, you may also use any letter of credit denial by sending in a copy of that letter within 60 days of its receipt with your written request. Be sure to include a copy of your state issued ID, proof of your address and your last known addresses for the past 5 years. It is very important to include a copy of your social security card.

What does it mean to have good credit? Who cares who sees it?

Unbelievably, your credit report is public information to anybody where you are asking for a line of credit. Any time you apply for employment, an apartment, or attempt to make a big purchase, you are asking for credit and permitting the potential creditor to view your credit report. Although your credit report does not reveal a personality diagnose, it may just as well, considering it is through your credit report how others (potential creditors) will perceive what kind of person you are.

Businesses look into your credit report and determine by your ability to pay and follow through on your promises what kind of person you are.

Do you adhere to your promises?

Are you stable, do you follow through on payments?

If so, then you most likely are a good and reliable person. You may be worth giving a chance at that perfect job, or residing in that particular community.

What about good people with bad credit?

You may be a good person, you may even be the most considerate and compassionate person alive; however, if your credit report shows a late payment or no payment on an account at all, your entire being could be perceived as not reliable, unstable and untrustworthy. Prepare yourself to deal with a lot of paper work and phone time once you are ready to repair your credit.

What does this mean? How can I protect my reputation?

What this means is that it is time for you to fix your credit. Your income may be null or limited, that's ok, there is still a way to save your personal reputation and open more doors of opportunity. Once you receive your credit report(s), contact the creditors listed and make payment arrangements, even if it is just $1-$5 a month. Doing this shows your willingness to get back on track, it show that you are putting effort towards establishing stability and responsibility.

Whom can I turn to for help?

There are many resources available to assist with credit repair, make use of your library or the internet. Most credit repair agencies offer free services, take advantage of their offers and assistance. Building your credit is more than being able to make a big purchase, it also means you are establishing your personal reputation and setting your survival foundation.

CHAPTER 2- THE MOST EFFECTIVE WAYS OF DEALING WITH BAD CREDIT

Because of the way credit scores are calculated, some actions you take will affect your credit score better than others. In general, paying your bills on time and meeting your financial responsibilities will boost your score the most. Owing a reasonable amount of money and being able to repay it will show lenders that you take your finances seriously and pose little threat of lost money. There are a few tips that, more than any other will boost your credit score the most:

Pay your bills on time

One of the best ways to improve your credit score is simply to pay your bills on time. This is absurdly simple but it works very well, because nothing shows lenders that you take debts seriously as much as a history of paying promptly. Every lender wants to be paid in full and on time.

If you pay all your bills on time then the odds are good that you will make the payments on a new debt on time, too, and that is certainly something every lender wants to see. Experts think that up to 35% of your credit score is based on your paying of bills on time, so this simple step is one of the easiest ways to boost your credit score.

Paying your bills on time also ensures that you don't get hit with late fees and other financial penalties that make paying your bills off harder. Paying your bills in a timely way makes it easier to keep making payments on time. Of course, if you have had problems making your payments on time in the past, your current credit score will reflect this. It will take a number of months of repaying your bills on time to improve your credit score again, but the effort will be well worth it when your credit risk rating rebounds!

Avoid excessive credit

If you have many lines of credit or several huge debts, you make a worse credit risk because you are close to "overextending your credit." This simply means that you may be taking on more credit than you can comfortably pay off. Even if you are making payments regularly now on existing bills, lenders know that you will have a harder time paying off your bills if your debt load grows too much.

The higher your debts, the greater your monthly debt payments and so the higher the risk that you will eventually be able to repay your debts. Plus, statistical studies have shown that those with high debt loads have the hardest time financially when faced with a crisis such as a divorce, unemployment, or sudden illness.

Get Your Loans Approved!

Lenders (and credit bureaus who calculate your credit score) know that the more debt you have the greater problems you will have in case you do run into a life crisis. In order to have a great credit score, avoid taking out excessive credit. You should stick to one or two credit cards and one or two other major debts (car loan, mortgage) in order to have the best credit rating. Do not apply for every new credit line or credit card "just in case." Borrow only when you need it and make sure to make payments on your debts on time.

You should also know that taking out lots of new credit accounts in a relatively short period of time will cause your credit score to nosedive because it will look as though you are being financially irresponsible.

Cut down Your Debts

If you have a lot of debt, your credit score will suffer. Paying down your debts to a minimum will help elevate your credit score. For example, if you have a $1000 limit on your credit card and you regularly carry a balance of $900, you will be a less attractive credit risk to lenders than someone who has the same credit card but carries a smaller balance of $100 or so. If you are serious about improving your credit score, then start with the largest debt you have and start paying it down so that you are using a less large percentage of your credit total.

In general, try to make sure that you use no more than 50% of your credit. That means that if your credit card has a limit of $5000, make sure that you pay it down to at least $2500 and work at carrying no larger balance. If possible, reduce the debt even more. If you can pay off your credit card in full each month that is even better. What counts here is what percentage of your total credit limit you are using - the lower the better.

Have a range of credit types

The types of credit you have are a factor in calculating your credit score. In general, lenders like to see that you are able to handle a range of credit types well. Having some form of personal credit - such as credit cards - and some larger types of credit - such as a mortgage or auto loan - and paying them off regularly is better than having only one type of credit.

How to Get Out/Avoid More Debts

There are essentials to repairing your credit and building your history. It depends on your situation, but in most cases you can find a way out of any debt situation. Debt relief is a stressful situation. When times are hard the last thing we need is to add more stress to our lives. Therefore we want to start out by acknowledging the problems in front of us. Once we acknowledge the problem we can take the next step to find a resolve.

Now that we have some essential steps to repairing credit, we next want to review some of the options available to us. There are many steps we can take to eliminating debt. Repairing your credit means that you must learn the different scams on the marketplace to avoid complicating your situation and adding to your debts.

Telemarketers that claim to get you out of debt in three minutes are obviously scammers that are trying to make a buck. Anyone that tells you they can help you get out of debt and charge you are fee are basically a source of scammers.

The best solution then for getting out of debt is learning to rely on you. Repairing credit has its good and bad essentials. The basic rule of thumb is to search a way that works best for your situation.

Get Your Loans Approved!

Today we are going to take a look at some of the good basics in credit repair.

If you are in debt and own a home you probably have insurance coverage. If so you might be able to take an advance payment against your insurance. Life Insurance Coverage may offer a payback solution after you have paid in on the plan for a length of time.

It might be wise to check out your policy to see if there is some type of disbursement plan available. If you are able to get a lump sum be sure to pay off your debts rather than spending your money freely. You may even want to check into your Home Mortgage agreement and the insurance coverage available.

If you are suffering debt problems related to injuries or even suffer a Terminal Illness some policies will make payments on your mortgage until you are back on your feet again. If you are off work due to unemployed as no result of your own then you may be qualified on your insurance policy a coverage that makes your payments until you are back at work.

If you don't have insurance coverage you might or you have insurance coverage that doesn't offer this options you may want to check with your lender to find out if there is a refinance loan available to you that offers lower monthly installments and lower interest rates.

If you get into another loan you want to make sure that you are not paying more than you already are. If you decide to take out a refinance loan make sure that you are aware of the upfront fees that often are included in mortgage loans.

What about car payments?

Are you paying a fortune on your car each month?

If so there may be an option that can get you some relief. You may be able to refinance your car, or else sell your car, making more money than what you owe on your loan. The extra cash can be spent toward a good used car. Sometimes used cars tend to last longer than newer cars and are less expensive to maintenance. Also, you could look into a repossession of the vehicle if your situation is out of hand. This will go against your credit report, but when there is no other solution sometimes we have to toss in the towel.

Finally, you can increase your income by selling valuable assets or else finding a job that pays more for your worth. Sometimes we work and are paid less than what we deserve, so if there is a solution available by all means jump on it.

Repairing credit has many essentials, but for the most part credit repair is just an illusion where many people do not take the step to repair.

Chapter 3- Maintaining Your Good Credit Rating

If you have a lower credit score that you would like, odds are that the score is caused by some small financial mistake or oversight you have made in the past. Not every person with bad credit has a low credit score caused by something they did, though. Sometimes, other people's criminal activity can affect your credit score. There are a few tips that can keep you and your credit safe form online and financial predators:

Watch Out for Identity Thieves

Many people who are careful about paying bills on time and having minimal debts are shocked each year to find that they have low credit scores. In many cases, this happens as a result of identity theft. Identity theft is a type of crime in which people take your personal information and steal that information to pose as you in order to get access to your accounts or identity.

For example, someone with your PIN numbers can remove small amounts of money from your bank account each month or someone can use your name and personal information to get credit cards in your name and use those credit cards with no intention of paying back the money. You are stuck with the large debts and the poor credit score.

To prevent identity theft, always check your account statements carefully each month. Report any suspicious activity or any charges you don't recognize at once. Also check your credit report regularly and immediately investigate any new credit accounts you do not recognize - this is the best way of detecting and acting on identity theft.

If you have been the victim of identity theft, report to the police at once and get a police statement. Send copies of this to your bank and credit bureaus. Better yet, get the credit bureaus to attach the report to your credit report, if you can. Close all your accounts and reopen new ones. You should not have to pay for someone else's illegal activity.

Practice Safe Business Transactions

To stay safe from identity theft, always follow safe banking and financial practices:

1) Keep account numbers and PIN numbers safe. Cover your account and PIN numbers when using debit at the store and refuse to give your PIN number to anyone. Avoid could fall into the wrong hands.

Get Your Loans Approved!

2) Only do business with businesses you trust.

3) If you get applications for credit cards in the mail that are "pre-approved" rip up the applications and enclosed letters before discarding them. No, this is not paranoid. Identity thieves sometimes go through garbage in order to find these forms so that they can fill them out and steal your identity.

4) If you use a computer, install good firewall and antivirus protection system and update it religiously. Better yet, take a course in safe computing at your local college or community center. You will learn many good tips for keeping all your information safe while you are online.

5) Never buy anything online from a company you do not trust of from a company that does not have encryption technology and a good privacy policy.

6) Even with all computer precautions, avoid providing private information through email or your computer. Be especially cautious if you get an email from your bank asking you to verify your information by clicking on a link - this is a popular scam that comes not from your bank but from criminals posing as your bank. Ignore the email and phone your bank about the message.

7) Be wary of unsolicited emails, phone calls, or mail advertisements. Most are from legitimate companies but there are companies who promise you a credit card over the telephone only to charge your existing credit card without sending you anything.

Similarly, letters will sometimes promise you specific items or services. Once you send in your credit card information (usually to a post office box) you hear no more from the company. If you need or want to buy something from a company, be sure to check the company's standing with the Better Business Bureau first.

Send a money order instead of a check (which had your account number) or your credit card information. If you do use a credit card, report any unusual charges or any payments you made for a product that did not arrive to the credit card company. In some cases, they can stop payment or refund your money as well as take steps to keep your credit card number safe.

8) Be wary of offers that seem too good to be true. If you get an offer for a ten million dollar check - for which you need to put down $5000 as a "sign if good faith"...if you get an offer for a free state-of-the art computer - if only you provide your account information... take a deep breath and consider before sending in your money and your information.

Offers that are too good to be true always are. Scam artists often rely on your belief in others and your trust to make money. They depend on the fact that you will be so excited about a product or service that you will throw good judgment out the window. Prove them wrong.

When faced with an offer that seems too good to be true, do some research on the web, through the Better Business Bureau, or ask the person making the offer some questions. Never take someone up on an offer that you have been given unsolicited unless the company and the offer both check out.

9) Read the fine print. Some services or companies will have tiny print in their contract or agreement that allows them to charge you extra hidden fees or that allows them to retract certain offers. If you get an offer through email or the mail, make it a habit to read the fine print.

10) Be alert for a sudden disruption in your mail service. If you do not get mail for some time, contact your post office and ask whether your address was recently submitted for a "change of address" service. It sounds strange, but it's true.

One way that criminals steal identities is to change your address at the local post office. They redirect your mail to a post office box number and steal your mail looking for personal information such as bank statements, pre-approved credit card applications, and other pieces of mail they can use to steal your identity.

They use this information to pose as you with lenders and run up huge charges in your name. Simply keeping an eye out on your mail can help you keep your credit score safe.

Keep a Watchful Eye on Your Credit Score

You are more likely to notice problems and inconsistencies if you check your credit score on a regular basis - at least once a year and preferably three times a year. Be sure to check your credit rating with each credit bureau, too. If you notice anything odd or anything you don't recognize (such as a charge account you did not open) report it immediately.

Sometimes, these errors are caused by mistakes made at the credit bureau, but they could be an indication that someone is using your identity. In either case, such mistakes could hurt your credit score. Fixing such errors improves your credit score. If you think you have been the victim of identity theft, take action at once:

Contact the three major credit bureaus and ask to speak to the fraud department. Explain that you have been the victim of identity theft (or believe you may have been) and ask that an "alert" be placed on your file. This will let anyone looking at your report know that you may have been the victim of fraud. It will also mean that you will be alerted any time a lender asks to look at your file - each time a lender does look at your file, it may be an indication that the identity thieves are trying to open a new account in your name.

When the lender sees that the person applying is not you, they will deny the thieves credit and in most cases the criminals will stop trying to access your identity. Most alerts on your file last 90 or 180 days but you can extend this period to several years by asking the credit agencies for an extension of the "fraud alert" in writing.

In some states, you can even ask for a freeze to be placed on your credit score and credit report which will prevent anyone but yourself and those creditors you already have from accessing your file. Any lenders the thieves contact to set up a new account will be refused access and the thieves will not be able to get any more money in your name. You are entitled to a free copy of your credit report if you have been the victim of identity theft. Be sure to take advantage of this offer so that you can check exactly how your credit has been affected. Dispute those items that are not yours.

2) Call the Federal Trade Commission (FTC) at 1-877-438-4338. This is the special hotline that the FTC has set up to help customers deal with fraud and identity theft. You will be able to get up-to-date information about your rights and advice as to what you can do to improve your credit score and keep in safe in the future.

3) Contact the police. Identity theft is a crime and you need to file a police report (be sure to keep a copy of this report) so that you can help the police potentially catch the criminals responsible. Contacting the police will also give you a paper trail and proof that a crime has been committed. Keeping a paper trail of the crime and your response will make it easier for you to repair your credit if it has been damaged by identity thieves.

4) Contact your creditors or any creditors that the identity thieves have opened an account with. Ask to speak to the security department and explain your predicament. You may need to have your accounts closed or at least your passwords changed to protect yourself.

You may also need to fill out a fraud affidavit to state that a crime has been committed - be sure to keep a copy of this form for your records. The security team of the creditors should be able to advise you as to what you can do. Be sure to note down who you contacted and when so that you have records of the steps you have taken to deal with the crime.

If you have been the victim of identity theft and you are deeply in debt to creditors you never contacted, you will not be held responsible for the charges - but you will have to prove that you have been the victim of identity theft, which is tricky since the thieves are using your name and claiming to be you. It is a frustrating experience because lenders will want to be paid and you will want to avoid paying for charges you did not run up. Being persistent and keeping good proof that you have been the victim of a crime will help to clear your credit score. In the meantime, however, you will be faced with a much lower credit rating than you deserve and you may have to put off larger purchases that may require a loan.

Do Not Commit the Same Mistakes to Keep Your Scores from Falling Again

There are a few things that people do without realizing it that have a bad effect on their credit score. Follow these tips to avoid the common traps that can sink your credit risk rating:

Beware of debts and credit you don't use

It is easy today to apply for a store credit card that you forget all about in three years - but that account will remain on your credit report and affect your credit score as long as it is open. Having credit lines and credit cards you don't need makes you seem like a worse credit risk because you run the risk of "overextending" your credit. Also, having lots of accounts you don't use increases the odds that you will forget about an old account and stop making payments on it - resulting in a lowered credit score. Keep only your used accounts and make sure that all other accounts are closed. Having fewer accounts will make it easier for you to keep track of your debts and will increase the chances of you having a good credit score.

However, realize that when you close an account, the record of the closed account remains on your credit report and can affect your credit score for a while. In fact, closing unused credit accounts may actually cause your credit score to drop in the short term, as you will have higher credit balances spread out over a smaller overall credit account base. For example, if your unused accounts amounted to $2000 and you owe $1000 on accounts that you have now (let's say on two credit cards that total $2000) you have gone from using one fourth of your credit ($1000 owed on a possible $4000 you could have borrowed) to using one half of your credit (you owe $1000 from a possible $2000). This will actually cause your credit risk rating to drop. In the long term, though, not having extra temptation to charge and not having credit you don't need can work for you.

Be careful of inquiries on your credit report

Every time that someone looks at your credit report, the inquiry is noted. If you have lots of inquiries on your report, it may appear that you are shopping for several loans at once - or that you have been rejected by lenders. Both make you appear a poor credit risk and may affect your credit score. This means that you should be careful about who looks at your credit report. If you are shopping for a loan, shop around within a short period of time, since inquiries made within a few days of each other will generally be lumped together and counted as one inquiry.

You can also cut down on the number of inquiries on your account by approaching lenders you have already researched and may be interest in doing business with - by researching first and approaching second you will likely have only a few lenders accessing your credit report at the same time, which can help save your credit score.

Be careful of online loan rate comparisons.

Online loan rate quotes are easy to get - type in some personal information and you can get a quote on your car loan, personal loan, student loan, or mortgage in seconds. This is free and convenient, leading many people to compare several companies at once in order to make sure that they get the best deal possible. The problem is that since online quotes are a fairly recent phenomenon, credit bureaus count each such quote estimate as an "inquiry."

This means that if you compare too many companies online by asking for quotes, your credit score will fall due to too many "inquiries." This does not mean that you shouldn't seek online quotes for loans - not at all. In fact, online loan quotes are a great resource that can help you get the very best rates on your next loan. What this information does mean, however, is that you should research companies and narrow down possible lenders to just a few before making inquiries. This will help ensure that the number of inquiries on your credit report is small - and your credit rating will stay in good shape.

Don't make the mistake of thinking that you only have one credit report

Most people speak of having a "credit score" when in fact most people have at least three or more scores - and these scores can vary widely. There are three major credit bureaus in the country that develop credit reports and calculate credit scores. There are also a number of smaller credit bureau companies.

Plus, some larger lenders calculate their own credit risk scores based on information in your credit report. When repairing your credit score, then, you should not focus on one number - at the very least, you need to contact the three major credit bureaus and work on repairing the three credit scores separately.

Don't make the mistake of closing lots of credit accounts just to improve your score

This seems like a contradiction, but it really is not. Many people think that to improve their credit score, they just have to pay off some debts and close their accounts. This is not exactly accurate. There are several reasons to think carefully before closing your accounts.

First, if you close an account you need (for example, if you close your entire credit card accounts) then you will have to reapply for credit, and all those inquiries from lenders will cause your credit score to actually drop.

Secondly, most credit bureaus give high favorable points to those who have a good long-term credit history. That means that closing the credit card account you have had since college may actually hurt you in the long run. If you have credit accounts that you don't use or if you have too many credit lines, then by all means pay off

Get Your Loans Approved!

some and close them. Doing so may help your credit score - but only if you don't close long-term accounts you need. In general, close the most recent accounts first and only when you are sure you will not need that credit in the near future. Closing your accounts is a bad idea if:

1) You will be applying for a loan soon. The closing of your accounts will make your credit score drop in the short term and will not allow you to qualify for good loan rates.

2) Closing your accounts will make your overall debt balance too high. If you owe $10 000 now and closing some accounts would leave you with only $1000 of possible credit, you are close to maxing out your credit - which gives you a bad credit rating.

In the short term, closing accounts will lower your credit score, but in the long run it can be beneficial.

Don't assume that one thing will boost your credit score a specific number of points

Some debtors are lead to believe that paying off a credit card bill will boost their credit score by 50 points while closing an unused credit account will result in 20 more points. Credit scores are certainly not this clear-cut or simple. How much any one action will affect your credit score is impossible to gauge. It will depend on several factors, including your current credit score and the credit bureau calculating your credit score.

In general, though, the higher your credit score, the more small factors - such as one unpaid bill - can affect you. However, when repairing your credit score, you should not be equating specific credit repair tasks with numbers. The idea is to do as many things as you can to get your credit score as close to 800 as you are able.

Even if you can improve your credit score by 100 points or so, you will qualify for better interest rates.

Don't think that having no loans or debts will improve your credit score

Some people believe that owing no money, having no credit cards, and in fact avoiding the whole world of credit will help improve their credit score. The opposite is true - lenders want to see that you can handle credit, and the only way they can tell is if you have credit that you handle responsibly. Having no credit at all can actually be worse for your credit score than having a few credit accounts that you pay off scrupulously. If you currently have no credit accounts at all, opening a low balance credit card can actually boost your credit score.

Never do anything illegal to help boost your credit score

It seems pretty obvious, but plenty of people try to lie about their credit scores or even falsify their loan applications because they are ashamed of a bad score. Not only is this illegal, but it is also completely ineffective. Your credit score is easy to check and not only will you not fool lenders by lying but you may actually find yourself facing legal action as a result of your dishonesty.

CHAPTER 4- THE EFFECTS OF YOUR CREDIT REPORT ON PERSONAL CREDIT

Lots of people have been denied loan, credit card or other form of credit because of wrong information the lenders find in their credit report. Before banks or any other financial institution grant your application for loan they will first find out about your credit history from bureau by requesting for your credit report.

Credit report is a compilation of your credit history, past financial transactions and personal information possible. This report is usually compiled by accredited agencies known as credit reporting agency.

Credit reporting agencies are organizations that help credit card companies, loan companies, banks, and departmental stores in the country to ascertain the credit worthiness of their would be clients. They provide these companies information about those who are good credit risk and those who are not. They receive most information about consumers from loan companies, credit card companies, banks, credit and lending sources. In this report you will their will be information on your occupation, place of employment, residence record, court and arrest records, income status, details on payment of your past and present bills and loans.

Once they have detail information from these sources, they give it to any organizations in need of it when requested. Though they keep on file information concerning you and your credit, they don't make final judgments as to your credit worthiness. The decision is up to the credit card companies or any lender which you are dealing with.

The credit score is used by banks, credit card companies, loan lenders and other financial companies to determine your credit worthiness. As a matter of fact, most lenders often based their charges on information in your credit report. Also, some employers often consider little information in your credit report before they employ you. If you have severe financial problems some will find it difficult to employ you.

Whenever you apply for new credit card, loan or any form of credit from any sources lenders will base their acceptance or rejection of your application on your personal credit report. If your credit report shows you've been reliable in the past, then you will most likely get the credit card or loan you apply for.

However, if you have in one way or the other defaulted on particular account or you were constantly late in making payments, it will likely be impossible for you to get the credit you applied for.

While compiling your report the agency or financial institution that's giving them the information may make mistake and give inaccurate information about your credit. If you did not dispute this error and demand necessary changes, they will leave it in your report. You can imagine the possible effects on your life in future. Because of this, it's very important that you check your report at least once a year

In other to be able to check your report for possible inaccurate information you have to request for a copy of your report. You can get a copy of this report from credit bureau because it's your personal credit file and you have absolute right to know what is in it.

You have right to know exact information they are giving out concerning your name and credit worthiness. If the report is not good enough or you can proof to yourself that it's all about your past, you can change it. You can build your new credit worthiness. It's possible.

CHAPTER 5- PRACTICAL TIPS ON CREDIT REPAIR

Home Improvement Financing

An awful credit borrower is at jeopardy to formulate an agreement. This is why, when he tries to get a loan again, probability is high that such a candidate will be given a tough time by the person lending; even though this time he gives some kind of a guarantee to pay back in time. Therefore, to get rid of this matter, the individual should solve the problem by going for particularly intended credit home enhancement credit, devoid of all the usual obstacles. This is available to the person who is borrowing and has had a poor credit history.

The cash that you get from this loan is for investing in some house upgrading work like making bigger rooms plus renovating your kitchen in a modern way and adding up some breathing space etc. In this way, you are not only using the loan in the right way but also enhancing the value of your home.

Get Your Loans Approved!

There are many tribulations for people who have credit miseries like payment failures, delayed payments, debts and district court rulings in their credit statement. Hence, for those people bad credit home improvement loan is an ultimate solution.

- What Is Bad Credit Home Improvement Loan?

Bad credit home improvement loan is a protected loan specified against the security of your house. Therefore, the person lending them has minimum risk and this is the reason for poor credit generally not becoming a roadblock while the bad credit home improvement financing approvals are sought. In case of such financing, the amount is easily available and the value of the loan is directly related to the value of your home, which undoubtedly means that borrowing bigger amount of this loan is very useful and handy.

- Advantages

Talking about advantages for this loan, the biggest one is that regardless of bad credit, the person still acquires home improvement loan at lesser interest price. Another benefit of this loan is that, it carries suitable repayment period varying between five and thirty years. This way you can decide to pay back the installment as supported by your repaying ability.

Before you submit an application for the loan, ensure that you have an error free personal credit account calculated properly. You should also be familiar with your credit score. Nevertheless, lest your credit count is short, you should pick up by paying off unproblematic debts and submitting an application for a better rate. Online lenders, banks and economic companies are the resource for the loan. While online bankers have a lesser rate than the other two, do keep in mind comparing online lenders for still lower rates for people with awful credit.

Secured Financing

The issue of higher interest rates has risen and it has become a key problem since the cost of buying a new home has become difficult for homebuyers. It is also difficult for people with bad credit to find mortgage for themselves. People with unfavorable credit record have an option of with bad credit secured loans, which has been prominent these days after the lenders have realized and supported the seriousness of the situation.

-Taking Guarantee

It is obligatory for the borrowers to present guarantee in the form of security that can be anything ranging from jewelry to home or any other precious thing that they own, if they are applying for the bad credit secured loans. This happens to be a basic condition. Nonetheless, home as a security is more favored in recent times. The total loan amount under the process of sanctioning to the borrowers is based on the assessment after the cost of the produced security has been properly evaluated and calculated. Largely, the amount of cash that has been granted for the loan is around £3,000. This quantity can go up to a huge number such as £75,000 at maximum level. The period for availing the benefit of the loan ranges from 5 - 25 years.

- Value of the Fund

The sanctioned fund can be invested on anything and it has no fixed value. Home enhancement and reconstruction, business founding, children's improved schooling, purchasing car etc., are few of the basic examples of poor recognition protected credits.

Nevertheless, the basic thing is that those people who take loans from others can employ and utilize the loan sanctioned money for paying off the amounts, which are due on them. Due to this, their extra earning or amount can come back to normal. In this whole process, there is no dearth of lenders for bad credits safe credits as the bazaar of money is filled with those people who let you borrow money.

Considering the bank account with respect to borrowers' purposes of safe instantaneous cash, loans available online is taken as the finest employing instrument nowadays. Presently, we can see many people who let other people borrow money from them according to their choices and circumstances. Those people, who let others borrow, reveal their own regulations and rules according to their own choice. This means that in order to escape from such irritating situation, it is required that at all times people should consume their important time while choosing a proper lender. Keeping that in mind, always go for those lenders whose rules and regulations are suitable with respect to your budget and those who offer you the best deal with respect to your choice.

Unsecured Loans

To the degree that we observe it, an individual who is in misery from an unfavorable credit record will certainly face a number of problems in receiving funds for his requirements. What people do not comprehend is that these are prospects that are in advantage to get hold of trouble-free finances. To benefit from the bad credit unsecured loans a guarantee is not always necessary in addition, this makes it much easier and simpler to achieve.

- **Easy to Get**

Getting hold of bad credit unsecured loans can be an extremely straightforward job, as the person borrowing is not necessarily required to engage any guarantee for the credit. As we need to guarantee with something to the lender, it becomes uncomplicated for borrowers like leaseholders and non-homeowners, since they do not include any positive feature to show and it is accessible for all types of people wanting to borrow. Prospective homeowners like people with debts or other bulks or with CCJs and IVAs who can't show their property as guarantee can also take up these unsecured funding.

Purpose of the Loan The individual can take these unsecured loans for any purpose as long as the need of the loan is fulfilling. The needs can be anything from home improvement to debt consolidation to wedding expenses and even educational funding. These loans also can be utilized for car purchase and travel expenses.

Improving Your Track

By timely payment of the loaned amount, the person borrowing can also improve the credit track and adding positive features to the credit history. In the course of this, the person borrowing can engage in total variation of £1000-£25000 for the requirements. Because of unfavorable record of the person, borrowing and guarantee-free temperament of the finance, the individual is requires to service the loan at a high charge of interest, yet a modest one. To benefit with lower interest rates, the individual can adopt a study online. This will help him evaluate all the arrangements that are accessible to him.

Get Your Loans Approved!

Currently, too many lenders are available online and are all set to lessen their charges of interest owing to the hard rivalry online. With this the borrower can benefit and take a decision about which loan agreement is the paramount for him. They offer a means to the person borrowing for developing their economic posture and advancing their credit record. Thus, bad credit unsecured loan happens to be a blessing in disguise for people with poor credit record and inability to offer security.

Debt Consolidation

Now this is an all-new kind of loan, which can solve many issues such as people with an awful credit history, or if someone is seeking to consolidate credit card or other debt, this loan is just suitable for them all. Whether one wants to secure credit card arrears or extra sorts of arrears, it can be devastating searching online heading to locate the paramount ones intended for your requirements and circumstances. Now this is a little outline of what sort of debt consolidation funding is accessible online.

You need to qualify for this loan as if any other loan to consolidate your debt or to use it in any way you want that you find suitable for you. If you boast of a house, you might be capable to obtain an impartiality loan using your evenhandedness or yet go more than the evaluated worth of your house to acquire the funding which you need. You can consolidate your arrears with a single little monthly compensation with no attachments to any of your personal property and this way you can be eligible for an unsecured finance that consolidates all your pending dues.

Some companies will help you supervise your loan with a single one devoid of having the necessity to use an additional loan, but frequently they charge you a bill and then they assist you by consulting for a lesser interest rate from your lenders plus managing your monthly expenses. Nevertheless, keep in mind that there are many companies and each has a different technique. Some techniques may help you save your cash and some are certainly worth the little monthly charge and these help you save to an extent more than what they charge.

There are several companies that are not genuine and acquire you the monthly installments with them and earn interest on the same, while you are at a loss as the nonpayment from their side results in late payments charges and penalty for you. These corporations can in fact charge you cash and make your circumstances worse. While searching for groups that help in getting bad debt consolidation loans, you need to be very cautious as to whom to work with. You need to be sure of their genuineness and reputation prior to making a deal with them.

Consolidating your arrears can supply enormous liberation and breathing space, when it is available with a single loan that is to be served instead of various non-payments resulting in poor credit standing.

Bartering System

Restoring Credit is Essential for surviving in today's time. Today's barter is moving back to the system as many people including business owners find it to be a solution for getting out debt or expanding their company. This might sound crazy, but if you think about it you can find a way to make money.

Barter means to exchange goods or services for equal value. However in some cases you can find people willing to exchange goods or services for less value. Bartering could even mean changing products or items for money. For example, if you have a bunch of Video games or a game system and in debt it might be wise to sell your game system and games, or trade it for something of more value to resell.

Some people out there want something that you have but can't afford it and are willing to exchange items for what they are wanting. If you can get a better deal to raise money how much easier can it get. If you have a lot of items in your home you can also sell your items on EBay, including the barter exchanges that you obtained. Reselling items to raise money to repair your credit might be the only solution available at times. Once you get into bartering and reselling you might find it an interest source for making money and start your own business.

The stars are at your limit. Be sure that you don't invest money into items that are not going to produce revenue. You could also raise money to repair your business if you have access to the Internet and can write. If you have good English skills it is possible to generate a small amount of income to make ends meet. Don't think that this is an alternative to work, rather keep your job and do your writing on the sidelines.

Most of the buyers on the market pay very little for articles, but in some cases you can make a lump sum that can pay off your bills. Credit repair is a job in itself. When you are trying to restore your credit it takes effort on your part. It also takes thinking since we often have to search for a solution to find a way out of debt.

There are many ways to generate money to repay bills. One way to generate money is to cut back on expenses. This is not as good as finding a barter system or selling system that will generate more income, but hey it works. One of the bartering systems that stuck out in my mind is when a woman told me about exchanging stickers, stationary, and other similar items.

The woman was able to generate a small amount of income, at the same time exchanging her ideas over the Internet. If you are able to connect to the Internet you might want to do a search to find out which services are available that can offer you a source of income that can get you on your feet.

The Internet is swarming with Spam so be very carefully before making a decision. Some services offer a small fee to get you a training package to help you start selling. EBay has a great package for $29.95, but be sure that you can market and sale before you commit yourself.

Another solution maybe trading your car for a more expensive vehicle and resell the car to pay off your creditors... This can happen believe it or not, but there are people out there that want something new and willing to downgrade to get the change. The world is filled with people of all sorts and sometimes we can get real good deals that can benefit us.

Regardless of your situation there is always a solution to survive and get out of debt. It makes no sense to rely on services and business that will only take your money, when there are options that can put you right into business while repairing your credit at the same time. Barter credit repair makes no sense until you come up with the solution for making money on your exchanges and using the money to repay your debts.

CHAPTER 6- DISPUTING ERRORS ON YOUR CREDIT REPORT

If you want to improve your credit score, you need to go right to the source - your credit report. Your credit report contains the information and data on which your credit score is based. If you can alter or update the information in your credit report, your credit score will change to reflect the alterations. For this reason, getting and checking your credit report is one of the first things you should do when you attempt to repair your credit score. There are a few tips that can help you deal with your credit report so that you can give your credit score a boost

Dispute errors on your credit report

Contact each of the three major credit bureaus - TransUnion, Equifax, and Experian - and get copies of your credit reports and credit scores. Carefully read over the reports and note any errors.

In writing, contact the credit bureaus and ask that mistakes be removed or investigated. This is called a dispute letter and once it is received, credit bureaus have to investigate your dispute within thirty days of receiving your letter. It is important to keep a copy of your letter and it is important to note the date the letter was sent. You should not be accusatory or abusive in your letter - calmly and clearly state the problem and request an investigation.

Note that you are aware the agency is required to investigate the claim within thirty days and note that you will follow up. Be sure that you do follow up with the issues you raised in your letter - just because the agency investigates does not always mean that your credit report will end up error-free.

Many credit bureaus now make it possible for you to correct errors on your credit report online - and many have information on their web sites that tells you exactly how disputes must be handled to be effectively removed. It is important that you follow this information exactly so that the inaccuracies on your credit report are removed promptly and your credit score is updated as soon as possible.

Add a note to your credit report if there is a problem you can't resolve

Sometimes, there are legitimate reasons why you didn't pay a bill. If a contractor refused to finish a job or did a poor job, then you may have refused payment, but the non-payment may still count against you on your credit report. If there are any unusual circumstances surrounding your credit report that may affect your credit rating - such as a case of identity theft - you can ask that a note be attached to your credit report to explain the problem. Some lenders will pay attention to this and some will not, but it is a better solution than nothing at all. Such a note will not affect your credit score but will affect your credit report. More importantly, it leaves a paper trail of the problem that lenders can look at if they choose.

Make sure you know who is looking at your credit report and why

Many inquiries look bad on your credit report, but more than that you likely want to know who can see your personal financial information, now that you know that your personal information is stored in a credit report. If you sign a document with a lender or apply for credit online, you can be sure that someone is looking at your credit report.

However, you may want to look over other documents in order to see who is taking a peek. Insurance agents will often look at your credit report, for example. Some landlords and potential employers will, too. You need to be careful about online sources, too. In general, when you provide someone with your social insurance number, you may be giving permission to look at your credit report. You shouldn't bar people from looking, but knowing who is looking is good financial practice.

Know the difference between soft and hard inquiries

When you pull your credit report to look at it, it is counted as a "soft inquiry." Only "hard inquiries" from lenders will affect your credit score dramatically. Although checking your credit score too often is an expensive habit, you should not avoid checking your credit report because you fear it will make your credit rating worse.

Contact creditors as well as credit bureaus when correcting inaccuracies in your credit report

When debtors find mistakes on their credit report, they often only contact the credit bureaus. While this is the most effective way to resolve the issue, you should in some cases contact the creditors whose account has caused a ding on your credit report. This can help future dings and resolve problems faster. Consider an example: Let's say that you were late sending a credit card payment two months ago because you were sick. The late payment is listed as a ding on your credit report even though you have paid it already. You should contact the credit bureau in order to get the error removed.

However, if you notice that the same credit card company has you listed as having late payments three months when you paid on time, then it is time to contact the credit company and ask how to resolve the problem. The information reported about you to credit bureaus should be accurate - if it is not, then the credit company should work to make sure that they correct the problem so that it does not happen again. You have an advantage in this - the credit company, unlike the credit bureau, depends on your business for their money.

This means that the credit company (or any other bill company presenting inaccurate information about you) is well motivated to correct the problem or risk losing you as a client. If you find that a company consistently reports inaccurate information about you to credit bureaus, consider making a formal complaint to the company about it or switch companies. There is no reason why one company's poor organization should cost you your good credit score.

Look out where you get your credit report - and what it contains

Get Your Loans Approved!

You can get your credit score from any number of resources. One place you can get it from is from credit bureaus themselves. You can pay for the service, but you qualify for one free credit report a year or qualify for a free credit report if you have recently been turned down for credit or if you think you may have been the victim of identity theft.

If you can, get a copy of your free credit report from each of the three major credit bureaus. If you can't get a free credit report, you should still try to get one, even if costs a few dollars. The savings you will enjoy on your loan rates when you improve your credit score will more than pay for the cost of the reports. There are a number of online companies that offer free online credit reports. These offers are very attractive because you get an online report without having to wait for a report to be sent to you, and you often can get several reports from the different credit bureaus at once, which can save you time.

However, these online companies vary widely, so you will want to compare a few different firms before choosing one. You will also need to read the online company's agreement very carefully - some promise free credit reports only with the purchase of a credit repair program or some other kit. In some cases, you can decline the offer and still get the report but in other cases you cannot.

Buyer beware.

Also, some companies will offer you free credit reports that are really a combination of reports from the three major credit bureaus. This is not useful, since you will want to compare each of the three credit bureau reports and fix each credit score separately. You will want to look out for online companies that offer credit reports that are very condensed and you will want to avoid companies that will spam you (send you unsolicited emails) trying to get you to subscribe to some service. Always read carefully to see whether the free credit report offer is legitimate.

That said, there are a number of online companies that offer credit reports and credit scores at no charge and these can be a useful way for you to start your credit repair, especially if you are comfortable around computers. If you don't qualify for a free credit report from the credit bureaus, a legitimate online company may be your best bet of getting your credit information so that you can start repairing your credit risk rating.

No matter where you get your credit score and credit report, make sure that you get the most complete information package you can. Credit reports are not very exciting or even easy to read. If you are ordering your report online, look for one that includes graphs or lots of details that are easy to understand. Make sure that you get both your credit report and your credit score - even if you have to pay extra. If you get just your report, you will not be able to follow the secret and complicated math formulas used to arrive at your score and the report itself will not make as much financial sense to you if you don't have your score in front of you, as well.

When you do get your credit report you will notice that it contains lots if information about you, including:

1) Your personal and contact information. This will include your name and your address, as well as your past several addresses, your social insurance number, your employers (past and present) and your birth date.

2) Your personal information about credit. A credit report notes all the details of your loans, including the types of loans you have now and have recently had, the dates these loans were opened, the credit limit on each loan, how well you have been repaying those

loans (this is important - skipped or late payments count heavily against you in your credit score), and who your lenders are.

3) Information about you that is on the public record. This may include bankruptcies, unpaid taxes, unpaid child support, tax liens, your dealings with collection agencies, foreclosures, loan defaults, civil lawsuits that you have been involved in, and other information. Much of this will stay on your credit report and will seriously affect your credit score.

4) Information about who has looked at your credit report and credit score. Every time that someone looks at your credit score it is called an "inquiry." Your credit report lists who has looked at your credit report in the past two years and how often you have applied for loans and credit in that period of time. Too many inquiries tend to look bad and tend to affect your credit score.

When you get your credit report, it is important that you look at all parts of your credit report and understand what you are reading. Mistakes in any area of your credit report can affect your score, so be sure to check the entire report for inaccuracies and errors.

CHAPTER 7- THE TRUTH ABOUT CREDIT REPAIR FIRMS

Credit repair companies are businesses outfits that offers debit consolidation loans, debt counseling, or debt reorganization plans that guaranteed to stop creditor's collection effort. One thing you have to know is that these companies are established to also make money so you need to be very careful when dealing with this people.

Though, if you are having trouble paying your bills, you may be tempted to turn to one of this companies that claims to offer assistance in solving your problem. Before you sign up with any of credit Repair Company you have to investigate them thoroughly. You have to really understand the services the business provides and what it will cost you before signing up with them. Make sure they have a written contract in place as well.

Most often the consumers that engage the services of most of this business do end up getting more problems. So it's very important that you check office of Better Business Bureau to be sure the company is not in problem already. If there has been a complaint about this company its better you do away with them.

Businesses offering credit repair services may charge substantial fees or a percentage of your debts and fail to deliver. Apart from that their fee will even add up to your debt making it more difficult for consumer to get out of debt. Though it's through that debt problem can be distressing, but you have to be careful when selecting a solution. Some solution providers don't do other things to add to your problem.

Despite the fact that U.S Government make it very clear that nobody can repair your credit except you, the credit repair companies keeps growing in number very blessed day. They will promise you heaven and earth just for you to buy their service.

One very important thing most people that are still taking the service of the credit repair companies don't understand is that government's advices are often based on advices of experts. They charge upfront fees, maintenance fees, and monthly fees, all of which you are supposed to place in a trust account.

Why should you in first place pay somebody to help you fix your credit, when it's obvious that most of their results are often temporary? You will end up losing more money.

When you use the service of credit repair companies to fix your bad credit you will be forced to share your personal information with them before they can do anything about your credit. The meaning is that you are liable to identity theft and unwanted mailings you did not solicit for from other companies trying to sell you something.

The whole truth is that you can do what most of these companies do, if you care to know how to do it. All most of them do is to write letters to credit bureaus, listing few information that are false in your credit report. When credit bureau get the information from repair company the will start investigating it.

They will remove the information temporarily during this period, thus giving you clean credit report. Since this report is temporary, if credit bureaus are able to proof their previous action right they will add it back to your report again. So if all you need is a temporary clean credit report, why not does it yourself instead of paying somebody to do it for you. It's obvious, nobody remove negative information that's accurate from your credit report.

Since you have legal right to obtain and dispute a copy of your credit report if there is any error in it, you can improve your credit more effectively on your own.

ABOUT THE AUTHOR

Kimberly is referred to as a "financial guru" because of her formal training and her exercises every day. Kimberly used to run a small private office for business but soon got it closed because of sanitation issues.

Today, Kimberly is a freelance business writer.

www.ingramcontent.com/pod-product-compliance
Lightning Source LLC
Chambersburg PA
CBHW051248170526
45165CB00004B/1616